WINE CELLAR
RECORD BOOK

*The house having a great wine stored below lives in our imagination
as a joyful house, fast and splendidly rooted in the soil.*

George Meredith 1828-1909

VIKING
an imprint of
PENGUIN BOOKS

Viking

Published by the Penguin Group (Australia)
250 Camberwell Road, Camberwell, Victoria 3124, Australia
Penguin Books Ltd
80 Strand, London WC2R 0RL, England
Penguin Group (USA) Inc.
375 Hudson Street, New York, New York 10014, USA
Penguin Books, a division of Pearson Canada
10 Alcorn Avenue, Toronto, Ontario, Canada M4V 3B2
Penguin Books (NZ) Ltd
Cnr Rosedale and Airborne Roads, Albany, Auckland, New Zealand
Penguin Books (South Africa) (Pty) Ltd
24 Sturdee Avenue, Rosebank, Johannesburg 2196, South Africa
Penguin Books India (P) Ltd
11, Community Centre, Panchsheel Park, New Delhi 110 017, India

First published by Penguin Books Australia Ltd, 2003

10 9 8 7 6 5 4 3 2

Text copyright © Penguin Books Australia Ltd 2003
Photography copyright © Simon Griffiths 2003

Cover design by Adam Laszczuk © Penguin Group (Australia)
Text design by Adam Laszczuk © Penguin Group (Australia)

Cover photograph by Simon Griffiths

Printed and bound in China by Everbest Printing Co Ltd

www.penguin.com.au

Wine

_____

_____

_____

Variety

_____

_____

_____

Vintage

_____

_____

_____

| Quantity purchased |
| Date |
| From |
| Price |

Date	Bottles left	Comments

Quantity purchased
Date
From
Price

$\mathcal{W}$INE

_____

_____

_____

$\mathcal{V}$ARIETY

_____

_____

_____

$\mathcal{V}$INTAGE

_____

_____

DATE	BOTTLES LEFT	COMMENTS

$\mathcal{W}$ INE

_____

_____

_____

$\mathcal{V}$ ARIETY

_____

_____

_____

$\mathcal{V}$ INTAGE

_____

_____

_____

$\mathcal{Q}$ uantity purchased
$\mathcal{D}$ ate
$\mathcal{F}$ rom
$\mathcal{P}$ rice

DATE	BOTTLES LEFT	COMMENTS

Quantity purchased	_Wine_
Date	
From	_Variety_
Price	_Vintage_

Date	Bottles left	Comments

$\mathcal{W}$ine

_____

_____

_____

$\mathcal{V}$ariety

_____

_____

_____

$\mathcal{V}$intage

_____

_____

_____

$\mathcal{Q}$uantity purchased
$\mathcal{D}$ate
$\mathcal{F}$rom
$\mathcal{P}$rice

Date	Bottles left	Comments

Quantity purchased

WINE

_____

_____

_____

VARIETY

_____

_____

_____

Date

From

VINTAGE

_____

_____

_____

Price

DATE	BOTTLES LEFT	COMMENTS

$\mathcal{W}$INE

$\mathcal{V}$ARIETY

$\mathcal{V}$INTAGE

$\mathcal{Q}$uantity purchased
$\mathcal{D}$ate
$\mathcal{F}$rom
$\mathcal{P}$rice

DATE	BOTTLES LEFT	COMMENTS

Quantity purchased	**W**INE
Date	**V**ARIETY
From	**V**INTAGE
Price	

DATE	BOTTLES LEFT	COMMENTS

$\mathcal{W}$INE
_____

$\mathcal{V}$ARIETY
_____

$\mathcal{V}$INTAGE
_____

| $\mathcal{Q}$uantity purchased |
| $\mathcal{D}$ate |
| $\mathcal{F}$rom |
| $\mathcal{P}$rice |

DATE	BOTTLES LEFT	COMMENTS

Quantity purchased	$\mathcal{W}$INE
$\mathcal{D}$ate	
$\mathcal{F}$rom	$\mathcal{V}$ARIETY
$\mathcal{P}$rice	$\mathcal{V}$INTAGE

DATE	BOTTLES LEFT	COMMENTS

$\mathcal{W}$INE

$\mathcal{V}$ARIETY

$\mathcal{V}$INTAGE

$\mathcal{Q}$uantity purchased
$\mathcal{D}$ate
$\mathcal{F}$rom
$\mathcal{P}$rice

DATE	BOTTLES LEFT	COMMENTS

Quantity purchased	$\mathscr{W}$INE
Date	$\mathscr{V}$ARIETY
From	$\mathscr{V}$INTAGE
Price	

DATE	BOTTLES LEFT	COMMENTS

$\mathcal{W}$ine

_____

_____

_____

$\mathcal{V}$ariety

_____

_____

$\mathcal{V}$intage

_____

_____

$\mathcal{Q}$uantity purchased
$\mathcal{D}$ate
$\mathcal{F}$rom
$\mathcal{P}$rice

Date	Bottles left	Comments

Quantity purchased	$\mathcal{W}$INE
$\mathcal{D}$ate	$\mathcal{V}$ARIETY
$\mathcal{F}$rom	$\mathcal{V}$INTAGE
$\mathcal{P}$rice	

DATE	BOTTLES LEFT	COMMENTS

$\mathcal{W}$INE

$\mathcal{V}$ARIETY

$\mathcal{V}$INTAGE

$\mathcal{Q}$uantity purchased
$\mathcal{D}$ate
$\mathcal{F}$rom
$\mathcal{P}$rice

DATE	BOTTLES LEFT	COMMENTS

Quantity purchased	$\mathcal{W}$INE
$\mathcal{D}$ate	$\mathcal{V}$ARIETY
$\mathcal{F}$rom	$\mathcal{V}$INTAGE
$\mathcal{P}$rice	

DATE	BOTTLES LEFT	COMMENTS

$\mathcal{W}$INE
_____

$\mathcal{V}$ARIETY
_____

$\mathcal{V}$INTAGE
_____

$\mathcal{Q}$uantity purchased
$\mathcal{D}$ate
$\mathcal{F}$rom
$\mathcal{P}$rice

$\mathcal{D}$ATE	$\mathcal{B}$OTTLES LEFT	$\mathcal{C}$OMMENTS

Quantity purchased
Date
From
Price

Wine

Variety

Vintage

Date	Bottles left	Comments

$\mathscr{W}$INE
_____

$\mathscr{V}$ARIETY
_____

$\mathscr{V}$INTAGE
_____

| $\mathscr{Q}$uantity purchased |
| $\mathscr{D}$ate |
| $\mathscr{F}$rom |
| $\mathscr{P}$rice |

DATE	BOTTLES LEFT	COMMENTS

Quantity purchased
Date
From
Price

$\mathcal{W}$ine

$\mathcal{V}$ariety

$\mathcal{V}$intage

Date	Bottles left	Comments

$\mathcal{W}$INE

_____

_____

_____

$\mathcal{V}$ARIETY

_____

_____

_____

$\mathcal{V}$INTAGE

_____

_____

_____

$\mathcal{Q}$uantity purchased
$\mathcal{D}$ate
$\mathcal{F}$rom
$\mathcal{P}$rice

DATE	BOTTLES LEFT	COMMENTS

Quantity purchased
Date
From
Price

Wine

Variety

Vintage

Date	Bottles left	Comments

$\mathscr{W}$ine

_____

_____

_____

$\mathscr{Q}$uantity purchased	
$\mathscr{D}$ate	
$\mathscr{F}$rom	
$\mathscr{P}$rice	

$\mathscr{V}$ariety

_____

_____

_____

$\mathscr{V}$intage

_____

_____

_____

DATE	BOTTLES LEFT	COMMENTS

Quantity purchased	$\mathscr{W}$ine
Date	
From	$\mathscr{V}$ariety
Price	$\mathscr{V}$intage

Date	Bottles left	Comments

$\mathcal{W}$INE

$\mathcal{V}$ARIETY

$\mathcal{V}$INTAGE

| $\mathcal{Q}$uantity purchased |
| $\mathcal{D}$ate |
| $\mathcal{F}$rom |
| $\mathcal{P}$rice |

DATE	BOTTLES LEFT	COMMENTS

Quantity purchased
Date
From
Price

Wine

Variety

Vintage

Date	Bottles left	Comments

Wine

_____
_____
_____

Variety

_____
_____

Vintage

_____
_____

Quantity purchased
Date
From
Price

Date	Bottles left	Comments

Quantity purchased	**W**INE
Date	**V**ARIETY
From	**V**INTAGE
Price	

DATE	BOTTLES LEFT	COMMENTS

$\mathcal{W}$INE

$\mathcal{V}$ARIETY

$\mathcal{V}$INTAGE

$\mathcal{Q}$uantity purchased
$\mathcal{D}$ate
$\mathcal{F}$rom
$\mathcal{P}$rice

DATE	BOTTLES LEFT	COMMENTS

Quantity purchased		$\mathscr{W}$INE
$\mathscr{D}$ate		
$\mathscr{F}$rom		$\mathscr{V}$ARIETY
$\mathscr{P}$rice		$\mathscr{V}$INTAGE

DATE	BOTTLES LEFT	COMMENTS

$\mathcal{W}$INE

_____

_____

_____

$\mathcal{V}$ARIETY

_____

_____

_____

$\mathcal{V}$INTAGE

_____

_____

_____

$\mathcal{Q}$uantity purchased
$\mathcal{D}$ate
$\mathcal{F}$rom
$\mathcal{P}$rice

DATE	BOTTLES LEFT	COMMENTS

Quantity purchased
Date
From
Price

$\mathcal{W}$INE

$\mathcal{V}$ARIETY

$\mathcal{V}$INTAGE

DATE	BOTTLES LEFT	COMMENTS

$\mathcal{W}$INE

$\mathcal{V}$ARIETY

$\mathcal{V}$INTAGE

$\mathcal{Q}$uantity purchased
$\mathcal{D}$ate
$\mathcal{F}$rom
$\mathcal{P}$rice

DATE	BOTTLES LEFT	COMMENTS

Quantity purchased		
Date		
From		
Price		

*W*INE

_____

_____

_____

_____

*V*ARIETY

_____

_____

_____

*V*INTAGE

_____

_____

_____

DATE	BOTTLES LEFT	COMMENTS

$\mathcal{W}$INE

_____

_____

_____

$\mathcal{V}$ARIETY

_____

_____

$\mathcal{V}$INTAGE

_____

_____

_____

$\mathcal{Q}$uantity purchased
$\mathcal{D}$ate
$\mathcal{F}$rom
$\mathcal{P}$rice

DATE	BOTTLES LEFT	COMMENTS

Quantity purchased
Date
From
Price

*W*INE
_____
_____
_____

*V*ARIETY
_____
_____
_____

*V*INTAGE
_____
_____
_____

DATE	BOTTLES LEFT	COMMENTS

$\mathscr{W}_{\text{INE}}$

$\mathscr{V}_{\text{ARIETY}}$

$\mathscr{V}_{\text{INTAGE}}$

$\mathscr{Q}$uantity purchased
$\mathscr{D}$ate
$\mathscr{F}$rom
$\mathscr{P}$rice

DATE	BOTTLES LEFT	COMMENTS

| Quantity purchased |
| Date |
| From |
| Price |

*W*INE
_____
_____
_____
_____

*V*ARIETY
_____
_____
_____

*V*INTAGE
_____
_____
_____

DATE	BOTTLES LEFT	COMMENTS

$\mathcal{W}$INE

_____

_____

_____

$\mathcal{V}$ARIETY

_____

_____

_____

$\mathcal{V}$INTAGE

_____

_____

_____

$\mathcal{Q}$uantity purchased
$\mathcal{D}$ate
$\mathcal{F}$rom
$\mathcal{P}$rice

DATE	BOTTLES LEFT	COMMENTS

Quantity purchased	
Date	
From	
Price	

*W*INE
_____
_____
_____
_____

*V*ARIETY
_____
_____
_____

*V*INTAGE
_____
_____
_____

DATE	BOTTLES LEFT	COMMENTS

Wine

Variety

Vintage

Quantity purchased
Date
From
Price

Date	Bottles left	Comments

Quantity purchased
Date
From
Price

*W*INE
_____

_____

_____

*V*ARIETY
_____

_____

_____

*V*INTAGE
_____

_____

_____

DATE	BOTTLES LEFT	COMMENTS

$\mathscr{W}$ine

$\mathscr{V}$ariety

$\mathscr{V}$intage

$\mathscr{Q}$uantity purchased
$\mathscr{D}$ate
$\mathscr{F}$rom
$\mathscr{P}$rice

Date	Bottles left	Comments

Quantity purchased	_Wine_
Date	
From	_Variety_
Price	_Vintage_

Date	Bottles left	Comments

$\mathscr{W}$INE

$\mathscr{V}$ARIETY

$\mathscr{V}$INTAGE

$\mathscr{Q}$uantity purchased
$\mathscr{D}$ate
$\mathscr{F}$rom
$\mathscr{P}$rice

DATE	BOTTLES LEFT	COMMENTS

Quantity purchased
Date
From
Price

_W_INE

_V_ARIETY

_V_INTAGE

DATE	BOTTLES LEFT	COMMENTS

$\mathcal{W}$INE

$\mathcal{V}$ARIETY

$\mathcal{V}$INTAGE

$\mathcal{Q}$uantity purchased
$\mathcal{D}$ate
$\mathcal{F}$rom
$\mathcal{P}$rice

DATE	BOTTLES LEFT	COMMENTS

Quantity purchased	*W*INE
Date	
From	*V*ARIETY
Price	*V*INTAGE

DATE	BOTTLES LEFT	COMMENTS

$\mathcal{W}$ine

_____

_____

_____

$\mathcal{V}$ariety

_____

_____

_____

$\mathcal{V}$intage

_____

_____

_____

$\mathcal{Q}$uantity purchased
$\mathcal{D}$ate
$\mathcal{F}$rom
$\mathcal{P}$rice

DATE	BOTTLES LEFT	COMMENTS

Quantity purchased
Date
From
Price

$\mathcal{W}$INE

$\mathcal{V}$ARIETY

$\mathcal{V}$INTAGE

DATE	BOTTLES LEFT	COMMENTS

Wine

Variety

Vintage

Quantity purchased
Date
From
Price

Date	Bottles left	Comments

Quantity purchased
Date
From
Price

WINE

VARIETY

VINTAGE

DATE	BOTTLES LEFT	COMMENTS

$\mathscr{W}$INE

_____

_____

_____

$\mathscr{V}$ARIETY

_____

_____

_____

$\mathscr{V}$INTAGE

_____

_____

_____

$\mathscr{Q}$uantity purchased
$\mathscr{D}$ate
$\mathscr{F}$rom
$\mathscr{P}$rice

DATE	BOTTLES LEFT	COMMENTS

| Quantity purchased |
| Date |
| From |
| Price |

Wine

Variety

Vintage

Date	Bottles left	Comments

WINE

VARIETY

VINTAGE

Quantity purchased
Date
From
Price

DATE	BOTTLES LEFT	COMMENTS

Quantity purchased
Date
From
Price

*W*INE

_____
_____
_____

*V*ARIETY

_____
_____
_____

*V*INTAGE

_____
_____
_____

DATE	BOTTLES LEFT	COMMENTS

$\mathcal{W}$INE

$\mathcal{V}$ARIETY

$\mathcal{V}$INTAGE

$\mathcal{Q}$uantity purchased
$\mathcal{D}$ate
$\mathcal{F}$rom
$\mathcal{P}$rice

DATE	BOTTLES LEFT	COMMENTS

Quantity purchased		
Date		
From		
Price		

*W*INE

_____

_____

_____

*V*ARIETY

_____

_____

_____

*V*INTAGE

_____

_____

_____

DATE	BOTTLES LEFT	COMMENTS

$\mathcal{W}$INE

$\mathcal{V}$ARIETY

$\mathcal{V}$INTAGE

$\mathcal{Q}$uantity purchased
$\mathcal{D}$ate
$\mathcal{F}$rom
$\mathcal{P}$rice

DATE	BOTTLES LEFT	COMMENTS

Quantity purchased
Date
From
Price

_W_INE

_V_ARIETY

_V_INTAGE

DATE	BOTTLES LEFT	COMMENTS

$\mathcal{W}$INE

$\mathcal{V}$ARIETY

$\mathcal{V}$INTAGE

$\mathcal{Q}$uantity purchased
$\mathcal{D}$ate
$\mathcal{F}$rom
$\mathcal{P}$rice

DATE	BOTTLES LEFT	COMMENTS

Quantity purchased
Date
From
Price

$\mathscr{W}$ INE

$\mathscr{V}$ ARIETY

$\mathscr{V}$ INTAGE

Date	Bottles left	Comments